The KidHaven Science Library

Hurricanes

by Peggy J. Parks

KIDHAVEN PRESS
An imprint of Thomson Gale, a part of The Thomson Corporation

THOMSON
GALE

Detroit • New York • San Francisco • San Diego • New Haven, Conn. • Waterville, Maine • London • Munich

For more information, contact
KidHaven Press
27500 Drake Rd.
Farmington Hills, MI 48331-3535
Or you can visit our Internet site at http://www.gale.com

LIBRARY OF CONGRESS CATALOGING-IN-PUBLICATION DATA

Parks, Peggy J., 1951–
  Hurricanes / by Peggy J. Parks.
    p. cm. -- (The KidHaven science library)
  Includes bibliographical references and index.
  ISBN 0-7377-3550-3 (lib. bdg. : alk. paper) 1. Hurricanes--Juvenile literature. I.
Title. II. Series.
  QC944.2.P37 2006
  363.34'922--dc22
                                        2005029952

Printed in the United States of America

Contents

Chapter 1

"It's Complete Devastation"

On August 23, 2005, a hurricane named Katrina began taking shape in the Atlantic Ocean. At first it was just a small cluster of thunderstorms that formed near the Bahamas. Then the cluster started to grow larger, developing huge, swirling clouds. Eventually it became powerful enough to be declared a hurricane.

Katrina struck southeastern Florida on the evening of August 25. It pounded coastal cities, and in the process flooded streets, destroyed homes, and killed more than a dozen people—yet its fury had only begun. Within hours of Katrina's first strike, the storm cut across southern Florida and headed out into the Gulf of Mexico. The gulf's warm tropical waters provided fuel for Katrina. This increased its strength and made it even more powerful. By the time the hurricane struck land again, it had grown into a howling, swirling monster.

A Drowned City

On the morning of August 29, Katrina slammed into the Louisiana coast. In the city of New Orleans, winds raging at more than 100 miles (161km) per hour knocked down trees and power lines, shattered windows, and ripped roofs off houses, stores, and schools. Cars and trucks were tossed through the air as if they were toys, and boats were flung across city streets.

This satellite image of Hurricane Katrina shows how enormous the storm was as it made landfall on the Gulf Coast.

is is a geographical reference

An emergency crew on a motorboat searches the flooded streets of New Orleans for survivors of Hurricane Katrina.

The mayor of New Orleans, Ray Nagin, had ordered that the city be evacuated. However, thousands of people did not leave. Many were poor and lacked transportation, so they had no way to escape. Others chose to ride out the storm at home. One resident who remained in New Orleans was Sam Morrison. In an e-mail sent to BBC News, he described the destruction and chaos caused by the hurricane, saying it seemed like the world was coming to an end. Morrison spoke of people running around the city, terrified and unsure what to do.

"Those who are leaving have clogged the roadways so extensively that little hope remains for those who have not yet decided to leave," he wrote. "Gas stations are breeding grounds for fighting and riots, as people are resorting to [violence] in order to get the precious gasoline they need to move their vehicles. This truly is the worst part of the storm and it only looks to get worse. God be with everyone who is trying to escape the madness."[1]

As Hurricane Katrina pounded New Orleans, conditions grew more dangerous because of the risk of severe flooding. The bowl-shaped city is below sea level and almost completely surrounded by water. For years, its only protection against floods was a system of large pumps and protective barriers known as **levees**. But hours of battering by Katrina's strong winds and driving rain proved to be too much for the levees. Some collapsed, and water started pouring into the city from Lake Pontchartrain, a large lake to the north of New Orleans.

Floodwaters soon turned the streets of New Orleans into rivers. Water gushed into homes, stores, and other buildings, forcing thousands of people to scramble for their lives. Bryan Vernon, a New Orleans resident who lived on the south shore of Lake Pontchartrain, spent hours stranded on his roof. Vernon screamed over howling winds, trying to get someone to hear him and save him and his fiancée. "I've never encountered anything like it in my life," he says. "It just kept rising and rising and rising."[2]

Another resident, Kioka Williams, managed to escape the raging floodwaters by cutting through the ceiling of the beauty shop where she worked. She describes her panic at the time: "We were screaming, hollering, flashing lights. It was complete chaos."[3]

Less than 24 hours after Katrina struck New Orleans, about 80 percent of the city was underwater. Hundreds of people drowned in the flood, including many who were trapped inside their own homes. Some people even died in health-care facilities. At St. Rita's Nursing Home, located east of the city, 34 elderly patients drowned when the building was submerged in the floodwaters.

Horrors in Gulfport

Other cities in the South besides New Orleans suffered as well. Winds of 145 miles (233km) per hour roared through Gulfport, Mississippi. More than three-quarters of the buildings in Gulfport were seriously damaged, and many were shattered into piles of rubble. At Harrison Central Ninth Grade School, the force of the winds collapsed a brick gymnasium. Windows were blown out of classrooms, as well as out of cars in the parking lot. The Marine Life Oceanarium, a home for dolphins, sea lions, and other ocean creatures, was completely destroyed. Some of its animals were swept out to sea.

Like New Orleans, Gulfport also suffered from severe flooding when waves towering 30 feet (9.1m)

Hurricane Katrina caused tremendous damage to businesses along the beachfront of Gulfport, Mississippi.

high blasted the city. Gulfport resident Mike Spencer was in his home when the flooding began. As the water rose rapidly around him, he used a surfboard to float from room to room. But the water kept gushing in, and he knew he had to get out. The water got so deep that he was forced to climb up to the attic—yet even that was not high enough, because the attic started to flood. Finally Spencer kicked out the wall and climbed a tree. He wrapped himself around a large branch and clung to it for four or five hours. As he waited to be rescued, he

A man sits on a Biloxi, Mississippi, beach among the ruins of homes demolished by Hurricane Katrina.

watched all the houses around him disappear beneath the deep, murky floodwaters.

In just a few hours, Hurricane Katrina demolished nearly the entire town of Gulfport. When fire chief Pat Sullivan surveyed the damage in his city, his reaction was one of emotion and shock: "Let me tell you something, folks. I've been out there. It's complete devastation."[4]

Unbelievable Destruction

Another city that was devastated by Katrina was Gulfport's neighbor, Biloxi, Mississippi. Gigantic waves slammed into Biloxi with incredible force. Those who witnessed the damage said it looked as though the city had been struck by a nuclear bomb. The hurricane demolished historic beachfront homes that had survived storms for decades. It also crumbled bridges and swept away shopping centers, churches, restaurants, and office buildings. Almost all of Biloxi's beachfront casinos were destroyed. One of them, the Grand Casino Barge, was lifted up from its moorings in the water and shoved across a highway.

One of Biloxi's worst tragedies occurred at Quiet Water Beach, a brick seaside apartment complex. The powerful force of the storm caused the two-story building to crumble, killing about 30 people. Witnesses said all that remained was a concrete slab surrounded by a pile of red bricks. Resident

Joy Schovest sobbed as she told reporters how she had fought for her life. "We grabbed a lady and pulled her out the window and then we swam with the current," she said. "It was terrifying. You should have seen the cars floating around us. We had to push them away when we were trying to swim."[5]

Tragic Aftermath

Katrina battered the Gulf Coast for less than a week—yet the death and destruction the hurricane left behind was immense. By the time it finally came to an end, it had killed more than a thousand people and caused over $125 billion in property damage. That means Hurricane Katrina was the most destructive storm in the history of the United States.

Chapter 2

Disasters of Nature

Hurricanes are considered the deadliest storms on Earth. They are so powerful, so destructive, and so violent that few natural disasters can compare to them. According to the National Aeronautics and Space Administration (NASA), during a hurricane's life cycle it "can expend as much energy as 10,000 nuclear bombs!"[6]

With waves as high as buildings and winds swirling at frightening speeds, hurricanes have the ability to wipe out entire cities. Tragically, that happened in September 2005 when Hurricane Rita struck Texas and Louisiana. By the time the brutal storm had blown over, all that was left of some areas were piles of splinters and bricks. Two Louisiana towns, Cameron and Creole, were demolished. The small fishing village of Holly Beach was completely destroyed. When the raging floodwaters subsided, there was nothing left—even the ruins had been swept away.

The Making of a Hurricane

Vicious storms such as Rita occur in tropical areas throughout the world. But they are not always called by the same name. In the Indian Ocean and Australia, the storms are called **cyclones**. In the western Pacific Ocean, the storms are known as **typhoons**. Only those found in the Atlantic and eastern Pacific oceans, the Caribbean Sea, and the Gulf of Mexico are known as hurricanes. The word is derived from Hurican, the name of an ancient Caribbean god of storm and fire.

No matter what the storms are called, they all form in the same way. They start with a thunderstorm known as a **tropical disturbance**. Such storms

A man rides his bike on a pier in Galveston, Texas, as powerful waves generated by Hurricane Rita crash around him.

develop over areas with warm climates where the ocean water is at least 80°F (27°C). Because the ocean is warmest between June and November, hurricanes are most likely to develop then. That part of the year is considered hurricane season.

The thunderstorm may remain small and eventually die out. Or it may grow into a tropical storm. At that point it is given a name by the World Meteorological Organization. The group uses different names depending on where the storm is located. These names help scientists track each storm's progress as it moves.

While the storm is forming, the warm tropical air causes great quantities of ocean water to evaporate. That changes the water into a gas called **water vapor**. As the air becomes saturated with moisture, it begins to rise. It is pushed upward by **converging winds**, or winds that bump into each other near the ocean's surface. The air cools as it rises, which causes the water vapor to change back into liquid form (clouds and rain droplets). This process, known as **condensation**, releases a great deal of heat energy. Hurricane researcher Chris Landsea says the storm acts like a huge heat engine, as he explains: "The 'heat engine' gets its energy from warm, humid air over the tropical ocean and releases this heat through the condensation of water vapor."[7] The force of this energy release is huge, and this is what drives the powerful winds of a hurricane.

The winds of a tropical storm spin around a column-shaped center point known as the eye. This spinning motion, called the **Coriolis effect**, is caused by Earth's rotation. As the storm continues to whirl, its eye acts like a giant funnel, sucking up moisture from the ocean. This causes more evaporation, followed by more condensation, which generates even greater amounts of energy. As the process continues to feed on itself, the storm grows bigger and stronger, with winds that spin faster and faster. Winds traveling from east to west (known as **trade winds**) push the growing, swirling storm across the ocean. As it travels, the warm ocean air keeps fueling it, making it even larger and more powerful. When the wind speeds reach 74 miles (119km) per hour, the tropical storm becomes a hurricane.

Hurricanes from the Inside Out

No matter how strong the hurricane becomes, the eye area remains calm. When the eye is passing over, people can be deceived into thinking the storm has ended—and that can lead to a dangerous situation. Hurricane Frances, which struck Florida in September 2004, had an eye that was more than 70 miles (113km) across. Governor Jeb Bush issued a warning to residents as Frances was moving toward their state: "It's an eerie feeling when

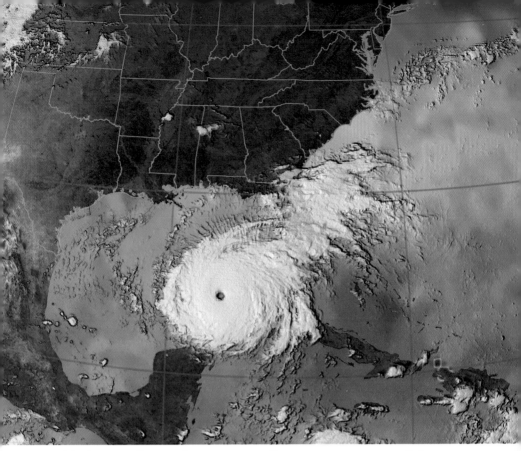

This image shows the warm surface temperatures of the Gulf of Mexico as Hurricane Rita passes over.

the eye moves over," he said. "There may be a false sense that the storm has passed. It could take about four hours for the eye of the storm to pass over you. Please don't take that as a sign that all is well."[8]

The area that circles the hurricane's eye is known as the **eye wall**. It is a tall, doughnut-shaped ring of clouds and thunderstorms. The eye wall is where the fastest, most violent winds are found. In 1969, when Hurricane Camille slammed into the Gulf Coast, winds in its eye wall were spinning faster than 200 miles (322km) per hour!

How Hurricanes Form

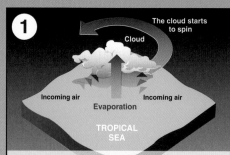

1

The cloud starts to spin

Cloud

Incoming air   Incoming air

Evaporation

TROPICAL SEA

Hurricanes originate in the tropics, where the water is warm and where the Coriolis effect is strong. Moisture rising from the tropical sea forms clouds. If winds are light, a mass of cloud can build up over one area. As the water vapor rises, the pressure falls and more air moves in. Under the influence of the Coriolis effect, the incoming air is deflected to the right and the cloud starts to spin counterclockwise.

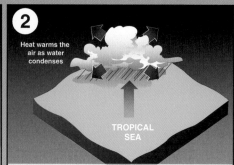

2

Heat warms the air as water condenses

TROPICAL SEA

The moist air cools as it rises into the cloud, and the water condenses out as rain. This releases heat, which expands the surrounding air and the cloud itself. More air is sucked inward and upward in a continuous cycle. This is known as a tropical disturbance.

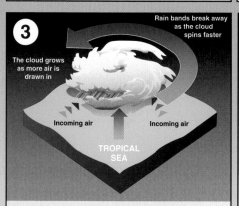

3

Rain bands break away as the cloud spins faster

The cloud grows as more air is drawn in

Incoming air   Incoming air

TROPICAL SEA

As the cloud becomes wider and deeper, the tropical disturbance becomes more organized and circular in shape.

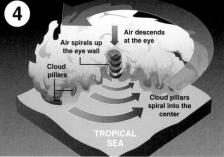

4

Air descends at the eye

Air spirals up the eye wall

Cloud pillars

Cloud pillars spiral into the center

TROPICAL SEA

Spiral bands of deep clouds with thunder, lightning, and heavy rain spin inside the tropical storm. At the center of the storm is the eye, a calm area around which everything rotates. As the rotating winds spin faster toward the eye, the Coriolis effect increases.

5

EYE

TROPICAL SEA

The process continuously builds if conditions remain stable. When sustained wind speeds reach 74 miles (119km) per hour, the tropical storm is officially designated as a hurricane. Typical hurricanes are about 300 miles (483km) wide with eyes between 12 and 37 miles (19–60km) across.

The outermost ring of the hurricane is made up of curved bands of clouds known as **rain bands**. They are sometimes called spiral bands because as they trail away from the eye wall, they form a spiral shape. Rain bands are capable of producing sudden bursts of heavy rains and strong winds.

Rating Hurricanes

Although all hurricanes form in the same way, there can be huge differences in their strength. When a storm changes into a hurricane, it receives an intensity rating. In the United States, the National Weather Service uses a classification system known as the Saffir-Simpson Scale. The scale rates hurricanes based on categories numbering from 1 through 5, with 1 being the weakest. Category 5 hurricanes are the most severe. Winds in a storm that powerful swirl at more than 155 miles (249km) per hour. A Category 5 hurricane named Gilbert that struck in 1988 had even stronger winds. When it smashed into the island of Jamaica, its winds were swirling about 180 miles (290km) per hour.

Powerful Weather, Huge Waves

The winds inside hurricanes spin extremely fast, but the storms themselves travel rather slowly. Most hurricanes lumber along at about 10 to 20 miles (16 to 32km) per hour, and some move even slower. As soon as they strike land, though, coastal communities start feeling their effects. One effect is heavy rainfall. In just a day or two, a large hurricane can dump dozens of inches of rain, which can lead to severe flooding. The spinning winds inside the storm can also be highly destructive. These winds can blow entire buildings apart. They can also uproot trees, wash away beaches, and toss vehicles as large as fire engines through the air.

One of the deadliest effects of a hurricane is the **storm surge**. This is a giant wall of water that smashes into the coastline when a hurricane strikes. Storm surges form as the hurricane's spinning winds push water into a mound at the center. The water continues to pile up and the mound grows taller and wider. Storm surges can grow to more than 30 feet (9m) high and 100 miles (161km) wide. An 1899 hurricane in Bathurst Bay, Australia, produced a storm surge that was 42 feet (13m) high—taller than a four-story building! When these enormous storm surges reach shore, they thunder over the land and destroy everything in their path.

Stronger Storms?

Most hurricanes last about nine days, but they are most destructive during their first twelve hours ashore. Once a hurricane moves over land, it starts to weaken rapidly. Without the ocean's moisture and heat, the storm no longer has the fuel it needs to grow.

The Saffir-Simpson Scale

The Saffir-Simpson scale is a way of grading hurricanes based on categories numbering from one to five. The intensity rating of a hurricane is determined by its wind speed and the damage it is likely to cause.

Category **1**

Wind speeds: 74–95mph (119–153kph)

Storm surge: 4–5ft (1.2–1.5m)

Some damage to trees, shrubbery, and unanchored mobile trailer homes

Category **2**

Wind speeds: 96–110mph (154–177kph)

Storm surge: 6–8ft (1.8–2.4m)

Major damage to mobile homes; damage to small buildings and roofs; trees blown over

Category **3**

Wind speeds: 111–130mph (179–209kph)

Storm surge: 9–12ft (2.7–3.7m)

Mobile homes completely destroyed; large trees blown down; buildings damaged

Category **4**

Wind speeds: 131–155mph (211-249kph)

Storm surge: 13–18ft (4–5.5m)

Extensive damage to fixed structures; ground floors near the coast likely to be flooded; major erosion of beaches

Category **5**

Wind speeds: Over 155mph (249kph)

Storm surge: Over 18ft (5.5m)

Extensive damage to all buildings; small buildings completely blown away; lower floors of buildings within 0.3 miles (0.5km) of the coast and less than 15 ft (4.6m) above sea level are flooded

Some scientists say that hurricanes are becoming fiercer than ever before because of warming ocean temperatures. During the past decade, the Atlantic Ocean has warmed about one to two degrees near the equator. Many scientists believe this is the result of a worldwide increase in temperature known as **global warming**. Whatever the cause, the warmer the ocean water becomes, the greater the amount of evaporation. So if ocean temperatures continue to rise, hurricanes could become more frequent—and more violent.

Chapter 3

Vicious Hurricanes of the Past

Hurricanes may be stronger today than ever before but they are nothing new. These vicious storms have plagued Earth for centuries. *National Geographic News* writer Willie Drye explains: "Sailors from Christopher Columbus to World War II admirals have had to contend with hurricanes. The storms have intervened in naval battles, spilled immense riches into the sea, shattered the grandiose dreams of real estate developers, and caused headaches for politicians."[9]

America's Deadliest Storm

One of those hurricanes from the past destroyed the town of Galveston, Texas, just over a hundred years ago. During the 1890s, Galveston grew from a small coastal settlement into one of the wealthiest cities in the country. The island city was home to about 37,000 people and was also a popular destination with tourists. Vacationers loved Galveston's sandy beaches, and balmy temperatures and the warm tropical waters of the Gulf of Mexico. But on September 8, 1900, a violent hurricane slammed into Galveston, bringing along with it 140-miles-per-hour (225km) winds and storm surges of nearly 16 feet (4.9m).

The people who lived in Galveston were caught off guard by the ferocious storm. There were no warning systems in place back then. One Galveston resident, meteorologist Isaac Cline, suspected something was wrong just before the hurricane hit. He noticed that the seawater was rising and the winds were becoming stronger than normal. Believing

Houses in Galveston, Texas, lie in shambles after a 1900 hurricane slammed into the town, killing thousands of people.

Teams of men use ropes to remove debris in search for survivors of the Galveston hurricane.

that serious danger was approaching, Cline rode up and down the beach on his horse to warn people. However, no one listened to his warnings—but even if they had, there was nowhere for them to go. The island was completely at the mercy of the hurricane. The massive storm surge moved over the island like a steamroller, collapsing houses and destroying everything in its path. Cline later wrote in his memoirs: "The battle for our lives, against the elements and the terrific hurricane winds and storm-tossed wreckage, lasted from 8 p.m. until near midnight. This struggle to live continued through one of the darkest of nights with only an occasional flash of lightning which revealed the terrible carnage about us."[10]

When the furious storm was over, survivors left their shelters to see what remained of their city. They were shocked and stunned at the devastation around them. Almost every building on the island was severely damaged, and nearly 4,000 structures were totally demolished. Blocks of coastal homes were flattened, replaced by piles of debris. Some houses had been swept off their foundations and tipped over onto their sides. The historic Sacred Heart Church lay in a pile of rubble.

The most tragic aftermath of the Galveston hurricane was the number of deaths. Somewhere between 6,000 and 8,000 people were killed. It later became known as the Great Storm of 1900, the deadliest natural disaster in the history of the United States.

Florida Tragedies

Another tragic hurricane from the past struck Florida in 1926. At that time, the state was in a period of rapid growth. Millions of Americans were lured to the Sunshine State in the hope of becoming rich by buying and selling land. Developers scrambled to build coastal cities where people could live. Then, in September 1926, a powerful hurricane smashed into Miami. Nearly all of Miami Beach was demolished by the storm. Hundreds of people were killed by the strong winds and widespread flooding. Drye explains what happened as a result of the hurricane: "When the winds finally stopped howling, thousands of terrified survivors scrambled aboard northbound trains and left, vowing never to return."[11]

Two years later, Florida was hit by another hurricane that was equally violent—and even more deadly. After striking Puerto Rico, the storm blasted Florida's

In 1926 a hurricane with winds strong enough to blow cars off the street struck Miami, Florida.

Atlantic coastline on September 16, 1928. It unleashed its fury on coastal cities from Fort Pierce to Palm Beach. However, the most devastating damage was to the tiny communities along Lake Okeechobee, 40 miles (64km) west of the coast. For about six hours, winds churned the lake and torrential rains poured into it. An earthen dike crumbled, sending a wall of water gushing onto farmland. The great force of the floodwaters washed homes off their foundations, uprooted trees, and swept animals and humans to their deaths. By the time the hurricane had blown over, as many as 2,000 people had perished. Journalist Liz Doup, who interviewed survivors 60 years after the storm, wrote about their terror: "It's the details—still sharp-edged after all these years—that shape the picture: how bone-chilling floodwaters swirled around their knees, how shrieking winds smothered cries for help, how pelting rain felt like needles piercing skin."[12]

Destruction and Death

As destructive as the Galveston and Florida hurricanes were, other storms in the past have claimed many more lives. For instance, the deadliest tropical storm of all time occurred on November 12, 1970. A powerful cyclone slammed into an area of Asia known as East Pakistan, which is today Bangladesh. Extremely powerful winds, coupled with a massive storm surge, devastated the heavily pop-

An image of Hurricane Mitch shows the tremendous size of the storm which ripped through most of Central America in 1998.

ulated country. Many people were killed in their sleep when the raging floodwaters swept their homes away. Although the exact death count will likely never be known, experts believe the 1970 storm claimed the lives of 300,000 to 500,000 people. Some officials have said the number could even be as high as a million.

A more recent hurricane known as Mitch proved to be the deadliest Atlantic storm in more than 200 years. In late October 1998, Mitch ripped through the

Central American countries of Honduras, Nicaragua, El Salvador, and Guatemala. The hurricane killed thousands of people and left millions of others homeless. Laura Arriola de Guity, a teacher from Honduras, was rescued after floating in the ocean for six days. When Hurricane Mitch struck her village, her family's house was destroyed. Her husband, her two sons, and her daughter were all swept out to sea in the floodwaters. She never saw them again. Although she was relieved to have survived, she said there was not much to live for: "I have nothing. I have nowhere to go. I lost it all."[13]

Wherever the hurricane went, it demolished roads and bridges, swept away electrical and telephone poles, and flattened thousands of acres of crops. As with the cyclone of 1970, the exact death toll from Hurricane Mitch will likely never be known. Government officials from Central America reported that more than 11,000 people were confirmed dead. More than 10,000 others remained missing long after the storm and will likely never be accounted for.

Almost anywhere hurricanes have hit, the storms have left death and destruction in their wake. Some have been worse than others, but all have proven to be awesome and powerful forces of nature.

Chapter 4

Storm Tracking

There is nothing scientists can do to stop hurricanes. Throughout the years, private companies and governmental agencies have studied ways to destroy or weaken the storms while they are in the sky. However, most have abandoned this idea as wishful thinking. Matthew Kelsch, a scientist with the National Center for Atmospheric Research in Boulder, Colorado, explains how useless such efforts would be: "It would be like trying to move a car with a pea shooter. The amount of energy involved in a hurricane is far greater than anything we're going to impart on it."[14]

Watching the Skies

Even though scientists can do nothing to control hurricanes, they continue to monitor and study them extensively. Their goal is to gain more knowledge about these storms. That includes how and why they form, when they are most likely to occur, and what areas are most threatened by them.

Organizations throughout the world monitor the activity of hurricanes and other types of tropical storms. The National Hurricane Center in Miami is responsible for monitoring and forecasting tropical storms in the North Atlantic Ocean, the Gulf of Mexico, and the Caribbean Sea. It shares responsibility for the northeastern Pacific Ocean with the Central Pacific Hurricane Center in Honolulu, Hawaii. Asian countries such as China, Thailand, Korea, Japan, the Philippines,

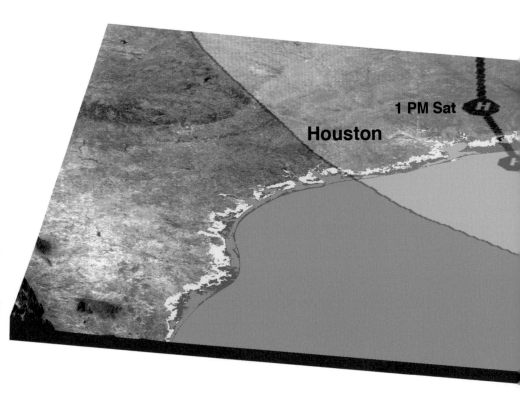

and Hong Kong, share forecasting duties for the northwestern Pacific Ocean. The Indian Ocean is monitored by officials in India, Pakistan, Bangladesh, Burma, and several countries in Africa. Tropical storm activity in the Southern Hemisphere is monitored by officials in Australia, Indonesia, New Guinea, and New Zealand.

This satellite image shows the path that weather experts expected Hurricane Rita to follow as it made its way to shore on the Gulf Coast.

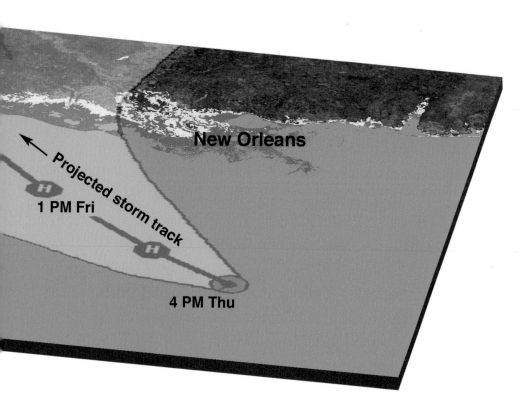

New Orleans

Projected storm track

1 PM Fri

4 PM Thu

Weather forecasters use highly sophisticated instruments to track tropical storms. These instruments are often housed on high-tech buoys. The buoys, which are monitored by the National Oceanic and Atmospheric Administration (NOAA), are as large as boats. They float in coastal and offshore waters from the western Atlantic to the Pacific Ocean around Hawaii, and from the Bering Sea to the South Pacific. They are equipped with instruments that can record air and sea temperature and wave height. They also have instruments to measure air pressure, wind direction, and wind speed. Antennae are mounted on top of the buoys. At least once every hour, the antennae transmit data to weather satellites that are in constant orbit high above Earth.

Monitoring from Space

The official names of the satellites are Geostationary Operational Environmental Satellites, or GOES. These spacecraft are able to monitor weather conditions all over the world. They have sophisticated cameras that can photograph and track air movements. They are also equipped with instruments that can gather different types of information about hurricanes. For instance, the satellites have sensors that can measure temperatures on land as well as on the surface of the ocean. They can also record information about water vapor at

Hurricane specialists keep a close eye on Hurricane Isabel in September 2003.

various altitudes in the atmosphere. They can calculate the speed of winds and measure amounts of precipitation. Their instruments are even sensitive enough to measure heat energy leaving Earth. As satellites gather this information, they beam signals back to monitoring stations on the ground.

The Hurricane Hunters

Forecasters depend on the information they receive from satellites to make predictions and warn people of approaching storms. But even more valuable to them is information they receive from U.S. Air

Hurricane Hunters use specialized planes in order to research hurricanes and collect weather data.

A Hurricane Hunter monitors the path of Ophelia aboard a research plane in September 2005.

Force reservists known as **Hurricane Hunters**. These brave people are scientists as well as pilots, and they fly WC-130 Hercules airplanes. Their job is to collect data that is either difficult or impossible to gather from observation stations on the ground, or even from satellites. During hurricane season each year, the Hurricane Hunters work for the National Hurricane Center. They scour the skies over the western Atlantic Ocean, Caribbean Sea, and the Gulf of Mexico, looking for tropical disturbances. In some cases they may fly missions over the northeastern Pacific for the Central Pacific Hurricane Center.

The Hurricane Hunters' airplanes are like flying laboratories. They are equipped with computers, radar equipment, and cameras. The planes also carry sophisticated weather sensors that determine the temperature, air pressure, wind speed, rainfall, and wind direction inside a hurricane. Other devices carried by Hurricane Hunters are called **dropsondes**. These are small tubes with instruments inside that can measure air pressure, temperature, humidity, wind speed, and wind direction. Dropsondes are equipped with radio transmitters and have tiny parachutes attached to the top. When the pilot is about 10,000 feet (3,048m) in the air, a crewmember drops the "sonde" from the plane. As it drifts through the eye of the hurricane toward the ocean, it takes measurements and transmits the data back to the airplane.

Each Hurricane Hunter mission lasts about eleven hours. If there is a hurricane, the pilots fly in and out of the storm four to six times. They monitor its activity by watching it from different altitudes. They also fly right into the center of a fully developed hurricane, which is a risky and highly precise task. A pilot must pierce the storm at exactly the right angle so the plane flies through the eye. One Hurricane Hunter describes this experience: "You go from blackness and bouncing all over the place and lightning to total calm conditions with blue sky and the sun. This kind of thing is pretty spectacular."[15]

When Hurricane Katrina was bashing the southeastern United States, Hurricane Hunter crews flew around the clock seven days a week. They were tracking the storm as it hit Biloxi. Some of them watched from the sky as their own homes and neighborhoods were destroyed. But as heartbreaking as that was for them, they remained committed to their

Survivors of Hurricane Katrina in Biloxi, Mississippi, ride their bikes past the rubble of homes just days after the storm hit.

task. Because of their efforts in monitoring Katrina and other violent storms, thousands of lives have been saved.

Sounding the Alarm

Information from Hurricane Hunters and satellites is transmitted to the National Hurricane Center. Meteorologists at the site use computers to compile and analyze the data. Special software helps them analyze a hurricane's intensity and determine the direction in which it seems to be moving. Then they make decisions about what types of warnings need to be issued, which is a very important responsibility. If they determine that there is a significant risk, they issue alerts to the local and national news media. If the risk is great enough, as with Hurricane Katrina, they may recommend that people in certain areas evacuate.

Hurricanes are natural disasters that cannot be stopped. They can, however, be closely studied so they do not catch people off guard. All the resources scientists use can help them gain a better understanding of hurricanes—and that could mean that fewer lives will be lost in the future.

Chapter 1: "It's Complete Devastation."

1. Quoted in BBC News, "Messages from Katrina's Path," September 4, 2005, http://news.bbc.co.uk/1/hi/talking_point/4206162.stm.
2. Quoted in Holbrook Mohr, "Katrina Leaves 80 Dead, Damage in the Billions," Live Science, August 25, 2005, www.livescience.com/forcesofnature/ap_050825_katrina.html.
3. Quoted in Jeff Goldblatt et. al., "It Is Not Safe in New Orleans," FOXNews.com, August 31, 2005, www.foxnews.com/story/0,2933,167781,00.html.
4. Quoted in Mohr, "Katrina Leaves 80 Dead, Damage in the Billions."
5. Quoted in Thomas Korosec, "Mississippi Search Crews Pulling Bodies from Rubble," *Houston Chronicle*, August 31, 2005, www.chron.com/cs/CDA/ssistory.mpl/nation/3332485.

Chapter 2: Disasters of Nature

6. NASA, "Hurricanes: The Greatest Storms on Earth," NASA Earth Observatory, http://earthobservatory.nasa.gov/Library/Hurricanes.
7. Quoted in American Red Cross, "Hurricane Awareness: How Do Hurricanes Form?" www.redcross.org/news/ds/hurricanes/010524ABCs.html.
8. Quoted in *News-Press*, "Slow-Moving Frances Continues Assault on East Coast," September 4, 2004, www.newspress.com/apps/pbcs.dll/article?AID=/20040904/NEWS01/409040463/1053/WEATHER01.

Chapter 3: Vicious Hurricanes of the Past

9. Willie Drye, "Hurricanes of History—from Dinosaur Times to Today," *National Geographic News*, September 23, 2004, http://news.nationalgeographic.com/news/2004/06/0607_040607_hurricanehistory.html.
10. Quoted in City of Galveston 1900 Storm Committee, "The 1900 Storm: Galveston Island, Texas," www.1900storm.com.
11. Drye, "Hurricanes of History—from Dinosaur Times to Today."
12. Liz Doup, "1928—Okeechobee: The Night 2,000 Died," *Sun-Sentinel*, September 11, 1988, www.sun-sentinel.com/news/weather/hurricane/sfl-1928-hurricane,0,2734526.story.
13. Quoted in BBC News, "Mitch Survivor: My Six-Day Ordeal," November 9, 1998, http://news.bbc.co.uk/1/hi/world/americas/210769.stm.

Chapter 4: Storm Tracking

14. Quoted in Joseph B. Verrengia, "Scientists: You Can't Modify Hurricanes," ABC News, September 22, 2005, http://abcnews.go.com/Technology/ wireStory?id=1149662.
15. Quoted in CNN Student News, "Quick Guide & Transcript—Hurricane Katrina, Hurricane Hunters," August 31, 2005, www.cnn.com/2005/ EDUCATION/08/30/transcript.wed/index.html.

condensation: The process of changing from a gas (such as water vapor) into a liquid as a result of being cooled.

converging winds: Winds that collide near the surface of the water.

Coriolis effect: The curving motion of anything, including wind, caused by the Earth's rotation.

cyclones: Violent tropical storms with rapidly spinning winds.

dropsondes: Small packages of instruments used to gather information about hurricanes.

eye wall: A ring of clouds and thunderstorms that circles a hurricane's eye.

global warming: The steady rise in the global climate.

Hurricane Hunters: A group of air force reserve pilots who fly airplanes into hurricanes to gather information about them.

levees: Protective barriers built along the banks of a river or lake to protect against flooding.

rain bands: Spiral-shaped bands of clouds that form the outermost ring of a hurricane.

storm surge: An enormous dome of water that builds up as a hurricane moves across the ocean.

trade winds: Strong winds that blow through the tropics in a westerly direction.

tropical disturbance: A cluster of thunderstorms that can grow into a hurricane.

typhoons: Tropical cyclones in the western Pacific Ocean.

water vapor: The gas that liquids change into when they evaporate.

Books

Jack Challoner, *Eyewitness Hurricane & Tornado*. New York: DK, 2004. This book uses stunning photography, eyewitness accounts, and real-life examples to help readers understand nature's most destructive storms.

Donna Latham, *Hurricane! The 1900 Galveston Night of Terror*. New York: Bearport, 2006. The story of the hurricane that struck Galveston, Texas, in 1900, killing more people than any other hurricane in American history.

Internet Sources

Renee Skelton, "Flying into the Eye of a Hurricane!" *National Geographic Kids*, September 2003. www.national geographic.com/ngkids/0308/hurricane/index.html.

Time for Kids, "Special Report: Hurricane Katrina," 2005. www.timeforkids.com/TFK/specials/articles/0,6709,1100404,00.html.

Web Sites

FEMA for Kids (www.fema.gov/kids). An informative site for kids that includes a whole section devoted to hurricanes.

How Stuff Works (www.howstuffworks.com). Lots of good information can be found on this site, including sections on how hurricanes work and how floods work.

The Hurricane Hunters (www.hurricanehunters.com). The official Web site of the U.S. Air Force reserve's Hurricane Hunters. Includes "Ask a Hurricane Hunter" and "Homework Help" sections especially designed for students.

Hurricanes: How They Work and What They Do, NASA Kids (http://kids.earth.nasa.gov/archive/hurricane). This site discusses how hurricanes are created, how they move, how dangerous they are, and the role of Hurricane Hunters in tracking them down. An interesting feature is a virtual reality tour of a hurricane.

Weather Wiz Kids (www.weatherwizkids.com). This excellent site, developed by New Orleans meteorologist Crystal Wicker, helps kids learn about weather-related phenomena in a fun and interesting way. In addition to hurricanes, there are also sections on tornadoes, wind, rain, floods, and earthquakes.

Picture Credits

About the Author

Peggy J. Parks holds a bachelor of science degree from Aquinas College in Grand Rapids, Michigan, where she graduated magna cum laude. An avid fan of all things related to science, nature, and weather phenomena, Parks has written more than 40 books for Thomson Gale's KidHaven Press, Blackbirch Press, and Lucent Books imprints. She lives in Muskegon, Michigan, a town she says inspires her writing because of its location on the shores of Lake Michigan.